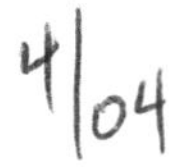

W9-DDJ-235

BETHEL PUBLIC LIBRARY
3 4030 09673 7371

Whitey Ford

Arthea Nolan

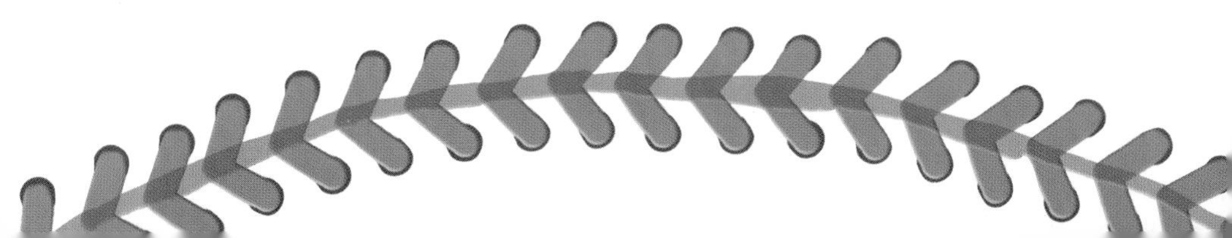

Published in 2004 by The Rosen Publishing Group, Inc.
29 East 21st Street, New York, NY 10010

First Edition

Library of Congress Cataloging-in-Publication Data

Nolan, Arthea.
Whitey Ford/Arthea Nolan.—1st ed. p. cm.—(Baseball Hall of Famers)
Includes bibliographical references (p.107) and index.
Summary: Describes the life and career of New York Yankees pitcher Whitey Ford.
ISBN 0-8239-3784-4 (library binding)
1.Ford, Whitey, 1928– —Juvenile literature. 2.Baseball players—United States—Biography—Juvenile literature.
[1.Ford,Whitey, 1928– . 2.Baseball players.]
I.Title. II.Series.
GV865.F6N65 2002
796.352'092—dc21
[B]

2002010758

Manufactured in the United States of America

Contents

New York Yankees legend Whitey Ford waves to the crowd on Whitey Ford Day, when he was honored for his fifty years of service to the team.

Introduction

At the age of seventy-four, Whitey Ford is still involved with baseball. Even though he has not played professionally since his retirement more than thirty years ago, he can still be seen coaching aspiring pitchers during spring training for the New York Yankees. He has been called "quite simply, the greatest pitcher to ever don the pinstripes" by former Yankee outfielder Bobby Murcer. Overcoming two bouts of cancer, Ford missed training for the first time in forty-nine years during the spring of 2000 due to the illness, but says, "I've been a Yankee for fifty-three years and I'll be a Yankee forever."

The man who was nicknamed Chairman of the Board for his command of the mental aspects of pitching and control was on the mound again at Yankee Stadium by August that

Ford, seen here on a baseball trading card, won ten of his twenty-two World Series starts, including two games each in three series. He was such a great pitcher that his manager Casey Stengel often referred to him as the money pitcher.

same year, throwing out the first pitch on Whitey Ford Day. Joining Ford in celebration of his half-century as a Yankee were eleven of his former teammates as well as his family. "It's been fifty years since I stepped on this field for the first time and it's still a thrill every time I come back," said Ford. "I've had some wonderful times. But this tops them all."

A native of New York City, Ford spent virtually his entire pitching career in a New York Yankee pinstripe uniform. During that time, Ford played in a total of eleven World Series championships, with the Yankees winning the title six times. Ford set numerous records during both the regular baseball season and during league and World Series championships, many of which still stand today.

Elected to the National Baseball Hall of Fame in 1974, Ford stands out among the Hall of Fame's list of pitchers for two reasons. First, he is one of just fourteen players to pitch with the left hand. And at five feet ten inches, his shorter height sets him apart. (Baseball pitchers are usually more than six feet tall.) But what Ford may have lacked in height he has more than made up for with his dedication to the game.

In 1974, the Yankees organization retired the left-handed pitcher's number 16, one of the team's fifteen numbers to be retired. Ford is the only Yankee pitcher to be honored in this way. Ford had the best winning record of any twentieth-century pitcher, with more than 200 victories. His longtime Yankee manager, Casey Stengel, once said of Ford, "If you had one game to win and your life depended on it, you'd want him to pitch it."

Ford, just twenty-one and still a rookie, gives the OK sign before starting the final game of the 1950 World Series at Yankee Stadium on October 7, 1950.

An All-Star Is Born

Whitey Ford was born Edward Charles Ford on October 21, 1928, in New York City, just a few miles away from Yankee Stadium. By the time he was five years old, Ford and his parents had moved to Astoria, Queens. New York City and the rest of the country were in the midst of the Great Depression, a period of economic hardship for many people. After the infamous stock market crash of 1929, many people lost their jobs. Money for necessities, let alone luxuries, was scarce. But Ford, the only child of hardworking parents, never really felt deprived as a youngster. Jim Ford, his father, worked for Consolidated Edison (Con Ed), a power supply service in New York. His mother was a bookkeeper for a chain of grocery stores, and later for the Equitable Life Insurance Company.

In the early years of the twentieth century, Astoria, Queens, seen here, was quite congested, and there were always enough kids around for a pickup game of baseball.

The neighborhood in which Ford grew up was made up of people whose parents or grandparents had come from Ireland, Italy, or Poland. Chiefly a Christian neighborhood, its social activities revolved around the Catholic Church. People lived in small apartment buildings or in one- and two-family houses. The entire neighborhood had a family atmosphere. "It was a close-knit community, kind of like one big family," Ford said in his first book, *Slick: My Life in and Around Baseball.* Children commonly played sports all year, especially stickball, football, and baseball. Ford credits his daily playing of neighborhood ball with preparing him for his future career as a major league player. As a kid growing up in Queens, he only dreamed about becoming a baseball star. "I never really thought I would make it because, as a kid, I always was too small," he said in *Slick*.

A Yankee Heritage

Ford grew up in the shadow of three great baseball teams—the National League's New York Giants and the Brooklyn Dodgers, and the American League's New York Yankees. Ford was a Yankees fan because his uncles rooted for the team and took him to games at Yankee Stadium in the Bronx. Young Eddie Ford went to his first Yankees game at age nine and saw his favorite player, Joe DiMaggio, pitch. "Little did I know that twelve years later I'd be on that mound [too]," said Ford in 2000 when the Yankees celebrated his fiftieth anniversary with the team. In the days when Ford was visiting Yankee

New York's Polo Grounds, once one of baseball's hallowed ballparks, was home to three baseball teams for more than half a century.

Stadium with his uncles, they would take the subway up to the Bronx, sit in the bleachers, eat hotdogs, drink soda, and watch baseball—all for less than one dollar.

The Yankees, in existence since 1903 when they were called the Highlanders, were three years younger than the other two New York teams. The team's popularity and success grew in 1920 with the signing of Boston Red Sox slugger Babe Ruth. In his first year with the Yankees,

Ruth hit a record-breaking 54 home runs, beating the record of 29 that he had set the previous season. By 1922, his popularity helped the Yankees finance the building of a new playing field in the Bronx. They moved from their shared field with the New York Giants—the Polo Grounds—to the brand-new Yankee Stadium in 1923, the same year the team won its first World Series championship. By the time Ford was born, the Yankees had won two more World Series titles, and the team roster contained more future Hall of Famers than did any other team's.

Eddie Ford continued to play baseball as he grew older, after school and on weekends. He and his friends played on public fields around an outdoor arena near his home. "When school was in session, we'd get to the field at about 3:15 PM and play until dark. On Saturday and Sunday, and during the summer, we'd be on those fields all day long, six, eight, or ten hours every day," he recalled in *Slick*.

When he was thirteen, Ford and his friends organized the Thirty-fourth Avenue Boys, a baseball team with uniforms provided by their parents. The team played in the Queens-Nassau League and was made up of amateurs, which meant that they were not paid. But there was always a possibility that one of these amateurs might get to play for a major league team. Staying with the team for five years, Ford expressed an interest in playing high school baseball. But because his local high school did not have a team, Ford and a teammate from the Thirty-fourth Avenue squad applied to the Manhattan School of Aviation Trades. They were both accepted.

A First Step

His interest in playing baseball and his abilities on the field earned Ford a place on his high school team at Manhattan Aviation, but attending the trade center did have its drawbacks. Living in Queens, Ford now had an hour-long bus ride to and from the school on the Upper East Side. And because his new high school was considered a vocational school, it did not prepare its students to go on to college.

Another disadvantage was that the school's baseball team played only teams from other vocational schools, many of them less talented than baseball players who attended academic schools. Finally, the team's home field was located under the 59th Street Bridge in Manhattan. As it received no sunlight, it had no grass. Homeless people often slept under the bridge and left empty bottles lying around, filling the play areas with broken glass. Before each practice, the team members scoured the grounds, cleaning the area for a game. But Ford

Ford played ball under the 59th Street Bridge, also known as the Queensboro Bridge, which connects Manhattan to Long Island City and Ford's neighborhood, Astoria.

stuck to playing baseball, securing the position of first baseman on the team. Increasingly, baseball became more important to him, especially because he was never considered a good student. "My schoolwork was terrible," he said in *Slick*. "I think the only reason I graduated was that I never missed a day of school . . ." The school's program was geared to training mechanics for the aviation industry, but, as Ford later explained, he had no interest in the field.

A Lucky Break

In the past, major league baseball teams regularly held tryouts for new players to join their minor league teams. If a player was good enough to join the major-league team, but needed additional training to sharpen his skills, he would be placed in one of the club's less well-known minor league teams. These clubs were based in different cities around the United States. For instance, at the time Ford was playing high school baseball, the Yankees had minor league teams in Pennsylvania, Virginia, upstate New York, and Missouri. Once signed by the Yankee organization, a player could work his way through the different leagues in the hopes that the major league club in New York City would eventually call him to play. A player who signed with a team in the minor leagues would be given much training and practice. He could sometimes learn to play more than one position so the team's coach could judge his strengths and weaknesses. Eventually, the most talented players would move on to the major league team, having spent a number of years gaining experience. In this way, major league teams always had athletes to fill their rosters if they experienced any shortage of players due to injury or retirement. That is why the minor leagues are also called the farm system—they are the "farms" where potential major league players are developed.

Specializing in the position of first base, Ford went to tryouts held by the Yankees in April of his senior year at Manhattan Aviation. He was

Ford worked hard to get to "the Big Show," which is what baseball players call the major leagues. He finally made it to Yankee Stadium, seen above in this picture from 1955.

given five pitches to hit and did poorly. But he did catch the eye of a scout hired to find new players for the team. That scout, Paul Krichell, asked Ford to throw a few pitches. He then instructed Ford on how to throw a curveball. (A curveball can often curve away at the last moment, causing the batter to swing at, but miss, the ball or to strike out.) Krichell thought that

Ford's pitching was his strength and claimed to have never seen an inexperienced player with such cultivated moves. Because Ford's talent came naturally to him, Krichell knew Ford could easily become a pitcher.

Ford returned to his high school baseball team and, that summer, to his neighborhood team. Although he had normally played in the first-base position, a shortage of players forced him to take over pitching duties. That summer, he posted his first wins as a pitcher. Playing in the Queens-Nassau League, the team was undefeated, with Ford posting a record of 18 wins and no losses. Winning the Journal-American Sandlot Championship game against a team from the Bronx, Ford was presented with a Most Valuable Player Award. After that game, he received calls from representatives of the Boston Red Sox, the New York Giants, and then the New York Yankees. Each of the teams was interested in signing Ford. He had quickly climbed the first step to becoming a major league player.

A Big Move

By 1947, major league baseball's interest in Ford was high. He had received proposals to sign with several major league teams. The Yankees, however, offered Ford the most money, though he later claimed that the team would have been his first choice no matter what the circumstances. After accepting, he was assigned to go to spring training with the organization's Binghamton club in the Eastern League. It was around this time that he received the nickname Whitey. Although it took some time to catch on, it became the name most people now recognize. His manager for that first training session was a man called Lefty Gomez. Gomez had so many new recruits to train that remembering all their names

As a pitcher for the Yankees in the 1930s, Vernon "Lefty" Gomez helped the Yankees win five American League pennants and five World Series championships.

proved difficult. Nicknames associated with the players' looks or their abilities solved the problem easily. Because Ford had blond hair, he was called Blondie or Whitey—the name that eventually stuck.

Ford had only been away from his home in Queens twice before, so moving was a big adjustment. He associated with other players during the spring and then was sent to play with the Yankees' Class C team in Butler, Pennsylvania. The team was a member of the Mid-Atlantic League. Although Ford liked what he was doing, he did not like the extensive commuting that came with it. Often, the team would sit on buses from ten to twelve hours a day traveling to and from games in distant cities. Still, Ford was pitching regularly as one of the team's roster of starting pitchers.

A starting pitcher is normally one of the main pitchers for a team, starting the game and ending it if possible. Starting pitchers have difficult jobs. They throw the baseball to batters, or the lineup, on the opposing team. In the course of a regular baseball game there are nine innings.

This structure gives each team the opportunity to put players from its lineup up to bat at least three times in a regular game, batting at least twenty-seven times per game. During each team's turn at bat during each inning, if three players strike out, or are tagged out, that team loses the chance to bat again until the next inning.

The pitcher has the first chance to put out the opposing side as he throws the ball and tries to strike out the batter. (In the course of an average game, pitchers can sometimes throw more than 150 fast-paced pitches.) The starting pitcher begins, and may end, the game. If his team wins, the starting pitcher may receive credit for that win—that is, if he has pitched at least five complete innings and his team is in the lead when he leaves the game. However, the manager of his team can remove him for different reasons. If this happens, a relief pitcher usually comes on to finish the game. If the team is not winning when the starting pitcher exits, or loses then regains the lead after he exits the game, the relief pitcher can claim the team's victory.

This photo, shot from just behind home plate, illustrates Ford's pitching power. He is firing a fastball to a batter during a game in April 1953.

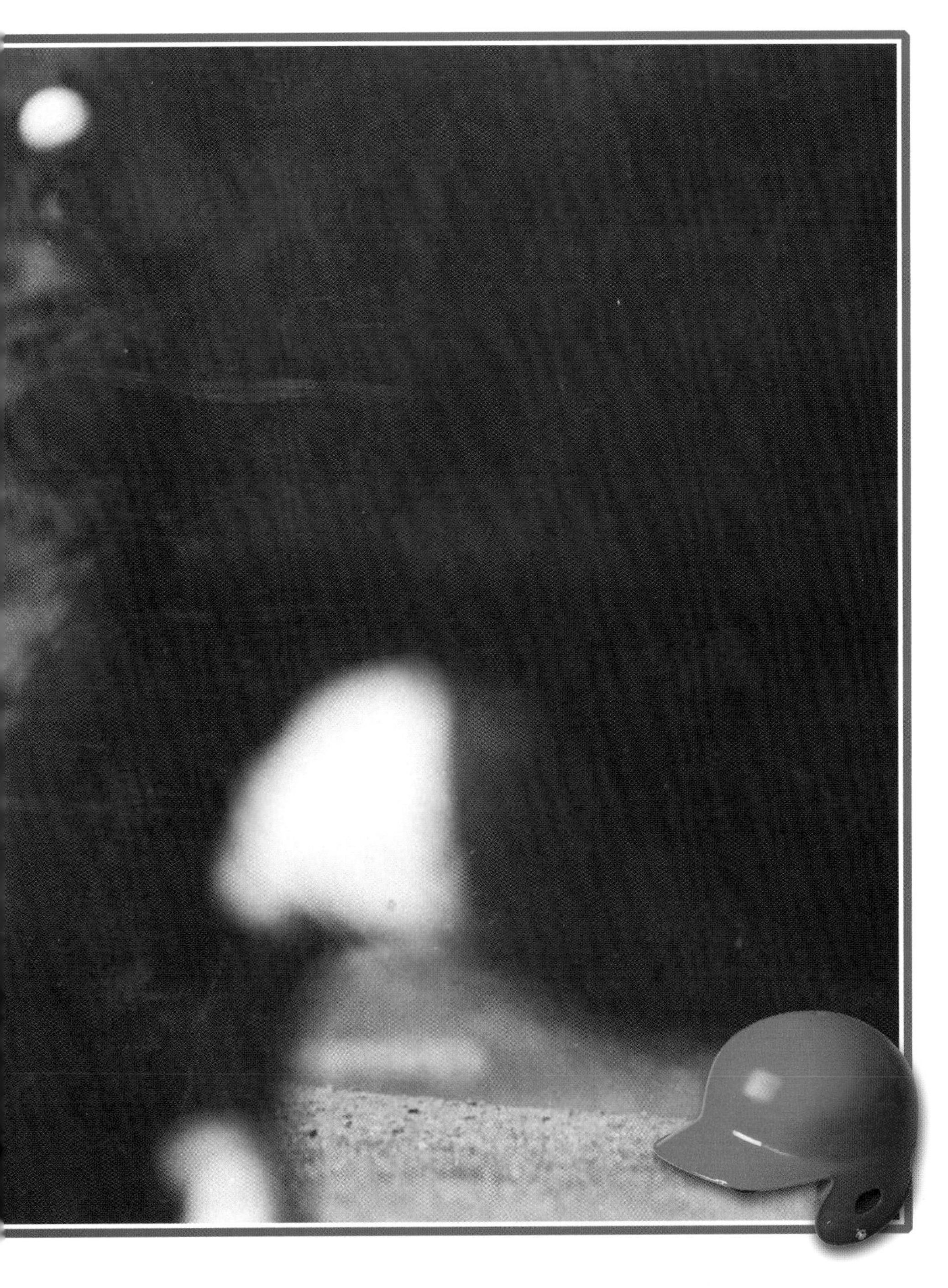

One important way of measuring a starting pitcher's success is to look at his win-loss record. In Ford's first year with the Yankees' minor league team in Pennsylvania, he won 13 games and had 4 losses. Another important statistic is the earned run average, or ERA, which represents the amount of runs a pitcher has allowed in a certain number of innings. (To find a pitcher's ERA, multiply the total number of runs scored by the opposing side by nine, and then divide that figure by the total innings pitched. The lower the number, the more skilled the pitcher is at keeping runs to a minimum.) Ford had an ERA of 3.84 during his first year in the minor leagues. The more Ford pitched, the more he strove to perfect his game. Working to control the balls he pitched, he used a combination of pitches, including the curveball and fastball. He was able to increase the number of batters struck out, proving to the team's management that he was ready to advance.

Moving Up

In 1948, Ford got that chance when he was sent to the Yankees' Class B team in Norfolk, Virginia. The Norfolk Tars belonged to the Piedmont League. During that year, Ford posted a 16–8 win-loss record and led the league in strikeouts with 171, an improvement over his first year. At the end of the season, Ford received an offer to play baseball with a Mexican club during the winter. Doubling his weekly salary of $200, coupled with the warmer climate of Mexico, he was delighted to go. He joined players from other American teams, including several from triple-A ball clubs that were closer to the major leagues than Ford was at the time. Mixing with these more experienced players gave him a boost of confidence.

But then, disaster struck. Ford became ill with an intestinal disease called amoebic dysentery. By the time the summer season was over, he had lost close to forty pounds. Although Ford was in no condition to play with his new team, the A class Binghamton Triplets, he began practicing anyway. Before the season had barely started, however, he again became ill. Now with a recurrence of his digestive problem, Ford was flown all the way back to a New York hospital where he spent more than two weeks recovering. By early May, he re-turned to finish the season with a 16–5 record. He also led the league with 151 strikeouts. Although his time in Mexico had given him some physical problems, he was able to overcome them to become a better pitcher. Ford's Binghamton team won the Eastern League Championship. Ford was now feeling stronger and even more confident. It was then that he first saw that it was possible for him to make it in the big leagues.

The Big Leagues

3

Winning a championship with the Yankees' Binghamton team was an important victory for Whitey Ford. Additionally, it showed the club's management that he could compete with—and win against—equally talented teams while under pressure. And early in 1950, Yankees management returned its enthusiasm for Ford's abilities by inviting him to spring training with the major league team. Ford spent a few weeks with the Yankees in their St. Petersburg, Florida, spring training camp. There, he joined players like Yankee batting legend Joe DiMaggio and catcher Yogi Berra. But soon Ford, as well as Yankee manager Casey Stengel, realized that he needed more preparation to play in the major leagues. He was sent down to the club's top farm team in Kansas City, Missouri, where he opened the season with a

6–3 record. He did not finish his baseball year in Kansas City, however. By July 1950, the Yankees had decided they needed another pitcher and recalled Ford to the team in New York.

Starting a game with the New York Yankees was an eventful occasion, especially for a native New Yorker and his family and friends. In mid-July, the first time Ford was starting pitcher in a game at Yankee Stadium, he gave more than fifty tickets to relatives and friends from his old neighborhood. After all, it was not every day that a real New Yorker pitched in a game for New York's most successful baseball team. Ford did not win that first contest against the Philadelphia Athletics, however, instead leaving the game with a tied score in the seventh inning. However, he did record his first win about four days later against the Chicago White Sox. In fact, for the rest of the regular season, he won 9 games and lost only 1. And then, for the first time in his career, Ford found himself doing what many young boys have dreamed of since the invention of baseball: He was playing in the World Series!

Ford readies for a game on March 1, 1953.

By early September, the Yankees were in first place in the Eastern Division of the American League. They had clinched the American League pennant by beating the Detroit Tigers and would face the National League's Philadelphia Phillies—the "Whiz Kids"—in the World Series. Considered tough opponents, the Phillies had a strong pitching staff and good hitters. But the Yankees were tougher. They won the first three games and needed only one more to win the series. Ford was named the starting pitcher for Game 4, which was played at home in Yankee Stadium. Barely four months into his first year as a major league ballplayer, Ford won the game, and the Yankees swept the World Series, earning their thirteenth world championship. And at the age of twenty-one, Whitey Ford was a World Series champ.

Duty to Country

After winning the series, Ford looked forward to a rest until spring training started in 1951. He was also eager to spend more time with his steady girlfriend, Joan Foran. They were both from the same street in Astoria, Queens, and had been dating for several years. Ford's future was about to change, however, and the Yankees were not going to be a part of it. At that time, young men were still drafted into the military as a way to fill the ranks of the armed forces in the United States. This meant that men over the age of eighteen, if eligible, were expected to serve for a set period. At the time, the United States was involved in the Korean War, and new recruits were needed to strengthen the country's defense. Ford was eligible for the draft, though he did not think he would be called. But barely a month after winning the World Series, Ford was summoned for duty to defend his country.

On November 19, 1950, he reported to his induction station in Manhattan. The prospect of two years in the army was a big surprise for the young ballplayer. "To say I was shocked would be a gross understatement," he said in his autobiography, *Slick*. Basic training, peeling potatoes, and long marches were not what the pitcher had in mind for the upcoming holidays. Besides the trauma of moving away from home, Ford faced an uncertain future. What if the

A newly discharged Ford carries a duffel bag and bats as he leaves the army barracks following two years of service to his country.

Yankees decided they could replace him? Or worse, what if his pitching skills waned after two years? Fortunately, he did not have to face those issues for very long. Once stationed at Fort Monmouth, New Jersey, Ford was given the assignment of playing for the camp's baseball team! Still, army life was rough, and Ford found himself pitching in three games a week. (Usually major league pitchers were accustomed to pitching one game a week, in order to give their throwing arms a rest.)

Now that Ford was able to practice baseball, he knew that he could maintain his skills until he was released from the army. And in early 1951, the Yankees showed that they had not forgotten their new pitcher. When Ford and Joan Foran got married on April 14, 1951, in Long Island City, New York, his entire team showed up after playing an exhibition game against the Brooklyn Dodgers. And on opening day several days later, Ford threw out the first baseball wearing his army uniform. His wedding day was a special day for another reason—it was the day he met someone who would later become his closest friend on the team. That man was future Hall of Fame slugger Mickey Mantle.

More Than a Brother

The first time Ford met Mantle, he thought he was a farm boy. Born in Oklahoma, Mantle was quiet and shy, so shy, in fact, that he spent Ford's wedding reception sitting on the team bus because he was uncomfortable around people. Mantle had recently joined the Yankees and was about to begin his rookie year with the team. Once Ford was discharged from the army in 1953, he rejoined the Yankees and the pair began to get acquainted. Although from different backgrounds—Ford was a city boy and Mantle hailed from the farmlands of Oklahoma—they became close through a mutual friend, Billy Martin. Martin, who would go on to manage the New York Yankees later in life, played second base. He had previously befriended the rookie Mantle while Ford was completing his military duty. By 1953, Ford came back to the Yankee team and the trio began spending time together, especially on Yankee road trips. Until Martin was

Ford holds the ball he threw out to start the 1951 baseball season at Yankee Stadium on April 17, 1951. Seated with him is his wife, Joan.

traded to the Kansas City Athletics in 1957, they became known as the Unholy Trio. They loved to play pranks on unsuspecting victims and were often seen socializing in New York nightclubs and bars. But to Ford, Mantle was more than a friend; he was the brother that Ford never had. "My greatest memories of him will always be the things we did off the field and the fun we had," Ford wrote in *Slick* before Mantle died of liver cancer in 1995.

4 A Return to Baseball

After Whitey Ford celebrated his release from the army in November 1952, the only uniform he was interested in wearing bore the famed navy-blue Yankee pinstripes. He was more than eager to pick up his career where it had left off in 1950, but he was worried about making the team after an absence of nearly two years. Despite his activities in the army, he was slightly overweight. "I didn't lose my stuff, but I didn't improve it either," he wrote in *Slick* about his pitching skills at the time.

Ford went to Yankees management to persuade them to sign him for the pitching roster. He stressed that his performance in 1950 was partly responsible for the team's World Series win. During Ford's spell in the army, however, the Yankees had won the World

Championship title in 1951 and 1952. Yankee management was not sure that they needed another pitcher, and Ford became concerned. He and his wife, Joan, now had a year-old daughter, Sally Ann, and were expecting another baby soon. Ford needed to provide for his family using the talent he had as a ballplayer. Later he regretted never pursuing higher education and considered himself very lucky for instead having had the chance to develop an athletic career. The Yankees did sign Ford to a contract that paid him $8,000 annually. Ford reported to his first spring training session since leaving the army and once again took up the life of a major league ball player.

Pitching for the Yankees in 1953, Ford wound up with an 18–6 win-loss record. He had more winning games to his credit than the other Yankees' pitchers. Once again, the team captured the American League pennant and was a contender for the World Series. The Yankees were pitted against their crosstown rivals, the Brooklyn Dodgers. Although Ford did not pitch

Ford winds up for a pitch in the fourth game of the 1950 World Series, which pitted the Yankees against the Philadelphia Phillies.

very well in that series, the Yankees beat the Dodgers in six games, after breaking a 2–2 tie at the end of Game 4. Ford had achieved his second world championship win and, along with the other team members, received a World Series check for more than $8,000. At the time, this was a great deal of money. For the first time in his marriage, Ford was able to put a down payment on a home, in Glen Cove, Long Island. The following year, 1954, the Yankees didn't make it to the World Series, but Ford pitched a decent record of 16 wins and 8 losses. His skill in controlling the ball was growing, and it looked as if he was destined to succeed. His family had grown, too. Joining Sally Ann were year-old Eddie, and now, a newborn named Tommy.

Controversial Call

By 1955, Ford was hitting his stride in pitching, and the Yankees were also doing well. During the regular season, Ford had won 18 games and had 7 losses. It wasn't surprising, then, when the Yankees won the American League pennant that year and were again set to play against their Brooklyn rivals. Ford was named to be the starting pitcher for the first game. His team hit well, and by the eighth inning the Yankees were leading 6 runs to 3, with Ford pitching. Dodgers player Jackie Robinson was at third base and looked as if he were going to steal home. Ford pitched the ball to his catcher, Yogi Berra, to tag Robinson out. Robinson reached home plate as Berra touched it with the ball in his glove. It seemed as if Robinson was clearly out, but the home umpire declared him safe—another run for the Dodgers. The Yankees won that game, 6 runs to 5, but many spectators insist that Robinson should have been out. Ford was equally adamant that his pitch to Berra was in time to secure the out. "To this day, I still believe that Jackie was out. I've seen the films of that play maybe fifty times, and Robinson is out every time," said Ford in *Slick*.

The Yankees won Game 2 of the series and began feeling confident that the team would achieve yet another world title. Throughout the history of the team, the Yankees had beaten the Dodgers five times in fourteen years. And as

Ford said, "No team had ever come back to win the World Series after losing the first two games." But the Dodgers *did* start winning. Playing on their home field, they won the next three games, and the series went back for Game 6 at Yankee Stadium—a game the Yankees needed to win to stay in the running—with Ford pitching. Ford's gift for performing under pressure served him well. After allowing only 4 hits, he won Game 6. Game 7, however, turned everything around for the Dodgers. They won by a score of 2–0 and earned their first world championship in their history. The Yankees vowed revenge.

The Champs' Comeback

The year 1956 meant another American League pennant for the Yankees. It also meant another meeting with the National League titleholders, the Brooklyn Dodgers, in the World Series. Ford had posted another good season, with 19 wins and 6 losses. As a result of his good performances during the year, he was once again named pitcher for Game 1 of the World Series at Ebbets Field, Brooklyn. He didn't like

Ford is shown pitching against the Brooklyn Dodgers in the seventh inning of a 1956 World Series game at Yankee Stadium in New York.

pitching in that ballpark, however, and his record there was poor. "I never pitched well in Ebbets Field because it was such a tiny ballpark with a short fence in left field and the Dodgers tailored their team to it," he explained in *Slick*. During that first World Series game in 1956, Ford allowed 5 runs and left the game in the fourth inning. The Dodgers went on to win the game, 6 runs to 3, and then went on to win Game 2 as well. The Yankees needed a win badly. Ford returned in Game 3 and, with the support of Yankee hitters, pitched a successful game, followed by another win.

Game 5 saw Yankee pitcher Don Larsen starting in Yankee Stadium. Not much was expected of Larsen, as he had been taken out of Game 2 in the second inning and the Dodgers went on to win the game, 13–8. But Yankee manager Casey Stengel decided to give Larsen another chance in Game 5. Although Ford spent most of the game warming up in the bullpen in the event that his services were needed, he could hear the crowd cheering. As things turned out, he wasn't needed. By the sixth inning, the Yankees had scored 2 runs, but the Dodgers had not even taken a hit off Larsen. Ford later wrote, "Larsen pitched the greatest game in baseball history that day. It was the only no-hitter ever pitched in the World Series. Not only that, it was a perfect game . . . You can't do better than that." On his way to becoming a great pitcher himself, Ford was both modest and generous enough to acknowledge great talent in others.

5 Winning and Losing

During the 1950s, the Yankees spent most of their time winning titles, often at the expense of the Brooklyn Dodgers. In that decade, the Yankees beat the Dodgers three out of the four times they met in postseason play. The Yankees were such a strong team at the time that they won every World Series from 1949 to 1953, a record that remains unmatched. And by 1957, Whitey Ford was considered the team's premier starting pitcher. Besides being nicknamed Chairman of the Board for his ability to control the ball to his advantage, he was also known to be a real "money" pitcher. That is, he was proficient in bringing home the wins for his team. By 1957, he was a veteran of the team, pitching when manager Stengel thought he could be more effective, mostly for the big games against tough teams such as the Dodgers and the Boston Red Sox. He was not in a regular rotation like most pitching squads are—pitching every three or four days and resting in between. Because Ford continued to perform well for the team, Stengel kept things as they were.

Pitching for the Yankees in 1957, Ford posted a record of 11 wins and 5 losses, and once again the Yankees won the American League pennant and were pitted against the Milwaukee Braves in the World Series. Named to start the series as the first game's pitcher, Ford was able to keep the Braves to 1 run, and the Yankees won the game, 3 runs to 1. But by Game 5, Ford was slumping. He was the losing pitcher of record for that game, and the Braves went on to win the series after seven games. Although Ford had followed a strict routine of training, he couldn't deliver the World Series crown in 1957.

A Year of Changes

The year 1957 was notable for another loss as well. During the season, Ford's close friend

Ford prepares to fire a pitch during Game 1 of the 1961 World Series against the Cincinnati Reds at Yankee Stadium.

and Yankee second baseman Billy Martin moved to the Kansas City Athletics. Supposedly involved in a nightclub brawl, Martin was considered a bad influence on other players by Yankee management, so he was traded. But Ford and some other players who were also involved in the incident were surprised by Martin's punishment. As Ford recalled in *Slick*, George Weiss, general manager of the Yankees, " . . . made Billy the scapegoat because he never liked him and was looking for an excuse to get rid of him." Ford became wary of Weiss and never cared for him much after that incident. Sad that one of his buddies was so far away, Ford had only his friend Mantle after Martin was traded.

At the conclusion of the 1957 season, changes in the baseball world were underway. Despite another trip to the World Series, attendance at Yankees games was dropping. Still, poor performance on the part of the team was surely not the reason for the lower turnout. After the 1957 season ended, two of New York's major teams left the city for the warm climate of California. Both the Dodgers and the Giants, former powerhouse teams of the National League, moved to Los Angeles and San Francisco, respectively. Ford often remarked that baseball, in New York at least, was never the same. Interest in the game there decreased because the sport had thrived on the intercity competition between the three rival teams.

Using His Head

Ford's pitching abilities seemed to diminish in 1957 as well. From 1957 to 1960, his combined win-loss record was 53–31, a performance that Ford admits was poor. Injury was cited as one of the reasons for his decline. As he later explained, many of his problems stemmed directly from injuries, although some of his peers expected that he was past his prime as a pitcher. Although professional pitchers usually peak in their thirties, Ford's talents seemed to be waning.

Ford had an active social life. He sometimes stayed out late with his friends and spent a good deal of time with his family when

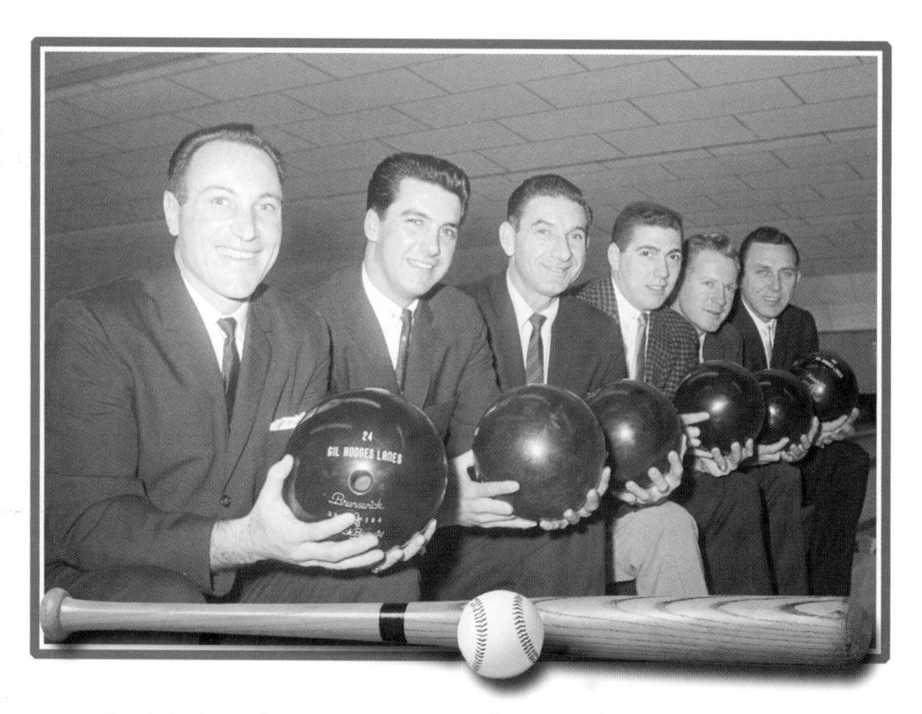

Baseball players line up to get some strikes in bowling instead of baseball in this photo from February 11, 1961. They are, from left to right: Joe Pignatano, Bobby Aspromonte, Sid Gordon, Bobby Giallombardo, Whitey Ford, and Gil Hodges.

not on the road. Still, he was always careful to keep up his pitching and conditioning routine. Eight hours of rest every night, hard throwing, and running were each a part of his regular physical training, but good pitching demanded more than physical ability. Ford would often study the opposing team during batting practice, occasionally noticing details that helped him gain an edge over opposing players. Observing batters and then using that information, he would often adapt his pitching style to thwart their chances of a hit. "You would be amazed how many important outs you can get by working the count down to where the hitter is sure you're going to throw to his weakness, and then throw to his power instead," he explained in *Slick*.

Ford concentrated on improving his statistics, and 1958 saw him winning 14 out of 21 games. The Yankees made it to the 1958 World Series, again playing against the Braves. Ford pitched Game 1 but wasn't involved in the decision that ultimately gave the Yankees a loss. He lost Game 4 and was taken out of Game 6 in the second inning. Some analysts of the game criticized Stengel for using Ford too often in the series with little rest. But the Yankees pulled together in Game 7, winning it and becoming world champions for the eighteenth time in the club's history.

The following season, 1959, was less memorable. Finishing in third place, the Yankees won only 79 games, the fewest number of wins for any Yankee team in thirty-four years. Although the team was not a series challenger that year, Ford was able to maintain a decent win-loss record of 16 and 10.

By the time 1960 rolled around, Ford was benched for the first six weeks with a shoulder injury. When he came back to pitch, he ended up with a 12–9 record. The Yankees won the American League pennant by 8 games over the Baltimore Orioles, and were scheduled to play the Pittsburgh Pirates in the World Series. It was at this point that Ford, and perhaps other members of the Yankees organization, began to question Stengel's leadership.

A Questionable Decision

As the Yankees prepared to play in the 1960 series, Ford expected to be named as the starting pitcher for Game 1. After all, he had been the starting pitcher for the opening games in the last two World Series. Considered by many to be the ace of the Yankees pitching staff, Ford was angry when Stengel instead selected a

The Pittsburgh Pirates' Bill Virdon takes the opening pitch from Ford in Game 3 of the 1960 World Series. The catcher is Elston Howard, and the umpire is Bill Jackowski.

different pitcher. Ford felt that he should have been the starting pitcher, giving him the ability to pitch three times during the series if needed. As it turned out, Ford didn't pitch until Game 3, by which time the Yankees and Pirates had won one game apiece. Ford shut them out on only four hits. The Yankees lost the next two games, however, partly due to their pitching. Slated to pitch again in Game 6, Ford prepared himself, intent on lifting the team's hopes with a win, thereby tying the series. Ford pitched Game 6 as a shutout, but couldn't impact Game 7. After reaching a tie score in the ninth inning of that game, the Pirates scored a home run off the Yankee pitcher and led Pittsburgh to victory. Later, Ford insisted that the game could have ended differently if he had been able to pitch sooner. "The reason I was so mad at Stengel for not starting me in [Game 1]," Ford said in *Slick*, " . . . I knew it cost me a chance to pitch three times in the Series. And the way I was pitching, I know I would have beaten them three times and we would have been world champs again."

Ford was confident enough in his own ability as a pitcher to believe that he could make a difference in every ballgame, a belief shared by his fans. However, not long after the loss of the 1960 World Series, Stengel was replaced as manager by former Yankees third base coach Ralph Houk. Despite being overlooked by Stengel as starter for the 1960

World Series, Ford was sorry to see him go as manager. "I feel privileged to have played for Casey Stengel, one of the great characters as well as one of the great managers of all time," he wrote in *Slick*. Ford played in eleven World Series championships, seven of which were decided in the crucial Game 7. Sadly, he did not pitch a seventh game in any of those series.

Ford stands with Yankee manager Ralph Houk (*right*), who led the team to world championships his first two seasons as manager.

A Golden Year

The first year of the new decade brought changes to the Yankee organization. General Manager George Weiss, never a favorite of Ford's, resigned. And longtime manager Stengel had departed from the team as well, shortly after a disappointing loss to the Pittsburgh Pirates in 1960. As Ford noted in *Slick*, " . . . the true measure of Stengel is his record with the Yankees—ten pennants and seven world championships in twelve years, including five straight world championships. No other manager has ever done that." But by 1961, the Yankees were about to see how certain changes to the team could still bring the world title. When talking about the season that was probably the highlight of his career, Ford often remarked that his greatest year as a pitcher actually started with a basketball game. At a St.

John's University basketball game in New York in January 1961, Ford ran into an old teammate from his early Yankee days. Ralph Houk, a Kansas native, had been asked to take over for Stengel. When Ford heard the news, he was happy because he believed that Houk could make a successful manager. Houk asked Ford if he would like to pitch in the upcoming season every fourth day. Without hesitating, Ford responded enthusiastically and a new partnership was formed.

The prospect of pitching in rotation every four days (instead of every five as he had done with Stengel), excited Ford. Under Stengel's fifth-day pitching rotation, Ford won 133 games and lost only 59. But the time in between games was a distraction. Ford never appreciated the long wait, finding it boring. He found watching the games even more frustrating. Houk brought in a new coach who encouraged the Yankees pitchers to throw the ball during practice and even in the bullpen during games. That way, pitchers could get in more workout time and learn new tricks. They built up their skills more than ever before. And the role of the relief pitcher was also becoming more important, as better closing pitchers like Ford's friend Luis Arroyo took command of the field.

A relief pitcher usually came into a game often after a starting pitcher had been able to secure a lead. He had to maintain that score until the end of the game to receive the "save." Arroyo was so strong a relief pitcher that starting pitchers could rely on him to hold that lead. Specializing in using a screwball pitch, Arroyo was able to win 15 games and save 29 in 1961. That made him tops in the American League for relief pitching. He was often partnered with Ford, coming in the seventh or eighth inning when the Yankees were in the lead to close the game. In this way, Ford was able to conserve his energy for his next starting game. The two played so often in the same game that the players would joke about it. "Who is pitching today?" one would ask and the response would be "Ford and Arroyo." Nevertheless, good relief pitching definitely helped to boost Ford's record in 1961.

Ford poses with Yankee pitcher Luis Arroyo on July 10, 1961. Arroyo began his major league baseball career in 1955 with the St. Louis Cardinals. He played for eight seasons on four different teams and ended his pitching career in 1963.

An Exciting Race

Although they are called one of the greatest teams in baseball history, in 1961, the Yankees spent most of the first half of the season in second place. But they blasted past other American League teams by mid-season and had sewn up the pennant by Labor Day. During this time, there were two players who contributed to many of the

Roger Maris *(left)* and Mickey Mantle were on one of the Yankees' greatest team rosters of all time. Though friends, Maris and Mantle could not have been more different. Mantle's social life was important to him, while Maris was quiet and dedicated to the game. Maris encouraged his friend to move in with him so he could more closely focus on baseball. When Mantle accepted, the media nicknamed them the M & M Boys.

victories won by the team. Ford's great friend, Mickey Mantle, and teammate Roger Maris spent most of the season pursuing Babe Ruth's single-season record of 60 home runs. The M&M Boys, as they were called, hit 115 of the Yankees' then-record 240 home runs. Ford was rooting for his best friend to win the race. Stating that Mantle had more "guts and desire" than any player he knew, Ford wrote in *Slick*, "I felt he was more deserving of the home run record because he was such a great player." But Mantle missed out on some games due to injury, ending the season with 54 home runs. Maris won the race with 61 runs on October 1. Two days later, the Yankees were playing Game 1 of the World Series against the Cincinnati Reds in Yankee Stadium, with Ford pitching. The team was determined to regain the championship after having been beaten by the Pittsburgh Pirates one year earlier.

Another Record Breaker

While pitching that first game, Ford allowed only 2 hits by a total of thirty batters. As a result the Yankees posted 2 runs, winning the game. But the win was important to Ford for another reason.

He had pitched two shutouts in the 1960 World Series in just two starts. The 1961 season represented Ford's third straight World Series shutout, though he did not know he was approaching Babe Ruth's record for consecutive scoreless innings in a season. (Ruth's record was

29 consecutive scoreless innings, set in the 1916 and 1918 World Series.) Ford had not thought before about breaking Ruth's record as it seemed quite difficult to reach and it wasn't such a big deal to him at the time. The Yankees lost Game 2 to the Reds and would have to travel to Cincinnati to play the next three. Although Ford, as well as other players, thought that the Yankees would lose the series, they won Game 3. Ford now had a chance to give his team the lead in the following game. He needed to concentrate on winning and possibly breaking a record in Game 4. If necessary, he could also pitch in Game 7 if there was one, something that he had never done before.

By the third inning, Ford had broken Ruth's record! He went on to pitch two more shutouts, extending his streak to 33 consecutive scoreless innings. But foul balls had hit him twice in the same spot on his foot during the third inning, and his foot began to swell by the fifth. Limping off the pitcher's mound at the end of that inning, Ford was finally taken out of the game. The team went on to win with a

Ford hoists the Cy Young trophy that he won in 1961 when he was named the most valuable pitcher in baseball.

score of 7–0. Ahead in the series 3–1, the Yankees had lost a number of key players, including Mantle and Berra, now out due to injuries. But they were still able to win Game 5—and the world championship. Ford credited the teamwork and quality of the players with this championship win. "Our extra men really won that Series and that's what made the 1961 team so great," he wrote in *Slick*. "We had so many good players who could come off the bench and do a job—players who would have been regulars on almost any other team." Finishing the season with an incredible 25–4 win-loss record, Ford was named winner of the prestigious American League Cy Young Award. He was ecstatic. The 1961 season had been an extra special year for Ford, likely thought of by himself and others as his best.

7 Celebrity Sightings

After the excitement surrounding the events of 1961 had calmed down, Whitey Ford had emerged as a celebrity in his own right. By now, the thirty-three-year-old pitcher had played in eight World Series and seven All-Star Games. He went to parties and dinners where he met famous people like the duke and duchess of Windsor and General Douglas MacArthur, as well as Hollywood celebrities Jackie Gleason, Elizabeth Taylor, and Betty Grable. Ford was famous and making a decent living to go along with it. Of course, the ballplayers of the 1960s did not receive the multimillion-dollar paychecks that some of today's athletes command, but Ford no longer needed to work during the off-season to make ends meet. He and his wife, Joan, were able to travel to places like Las Vegas, Hawaii, and even Japan.

But Ford was not such a big star that he forgot his roots. Living in Long Island, he was able to visit his old neighborhood in Queens, where some of his wife's family still lived. One story he tells shows how committed he was to his old neighborhood. Driving home from a sportswriters' dinner in Boston, Ford and Yankee teammates Mantle, Maris, and Elston Howard got caught in a snowstorm. Ford talked the men into stopping at the bar his father-in-law owned in Astoria. Well-known at the establishment, Ford's presence was not really surprising to the bar's regular customers. But his famous friends, placing $100 bills on the bar to buy drinks for everyone, stood out. Ford later recalled that his father-in-law's regulars were shocked. While the patrons were accustomed to seeing Ford stop by from time to time, they were surprised to meet Mantle, Maris, and Howard.

In 1962, the Yankees won 96 games in the regular season, less than their 109 wins in 1961, but still enough to get to the World Series again. Seeing the Yankees represent the American League in the world championships was expected by fans and teammates alike. Many fans took it for granted that there would always be baseball in October if the Yankees were playing. Once again, Ford was named starting pitcher for Game 1. The team was playing against the San Francisco Giants, formerly of New York. Ford won the first game, 6–2. It was the last of the record-breaking ten World Series victories for the left-hander. He pitched in Game 4, but left while the score was still tied. By the beginning of Game 6, the series was 3–2 in favor of the Yankees. On only one day of rest, Ford was brought back to pitch. Unfortunately, the Giants hit well, Ford was taken out in less than five innings, and the Yankees lost the game, forcing another Game 7. They redeemed themselves in that last game, however, and kept the Giants from scoring. The 1962 World Series crown again belonged to the Yankees.

Another World Series

The following year, 1963, Ford had 24 wins and 7 losses. He described it as his second-best year, citing his manager's three-day pitching rotation as one of the reasons for his good performance. The Yankees, who had captured the American League pennant, were scheduled to play their old New York rivals, the Dodgers. By now, the Dodgers had moved to California, and the team was well known for its excellent pitching. Ford and the rest of the Yankees prepared themselves. Pitching in Game 1, Ford encountered some tough batters, including one who was able to hit a three-run homer. The Yankees lost that game and the one that followed.

They traveled to California for Game 3, but the Yankees could only manage 3 hits and no runs. It was up to Ford to keep the team alive in Game 4. He started well, keeping the Dodgers to only one run. Tied by the end of the seventh inning, Ford and the Yankees were sure they had a shot at winning. But during the last inning with one man on third base, a Dodgers' batter hit a fly ball, the third

Ford greets rival pitcher Sandy Koufax *(left)* of the Los Angeles Dodgers before the two started Game 4 of the 1963 World Series.

baseman ran home, and the game ended. The Dodgers, formerly of Brooklyn, had swept the Yankees in just four games. "That's the worst I ever felt after a World Series," wrote Ford dejectedly in *Slick*. "The one consolation we had was that if we had to be swept by the Dodgers, at least it happened when they were three thousand miles away."

A Slow Decline

At the end of the 1963 season, Ford's contract was up for renewal. At that point, baseball had not yet reached the stage of signing players to multiyear, multimillion dollar contracts. Ford was simply called into the general manager's office and told how much his raise was to be that year—a sum of $12,000—making his new annual salary $76,000, a figure that remained the same until the year he retired. At the same time, the team was getting used to the idea of a new manager. Ralph Houk had moved up to the Yankees front office and selected Ford's old friend and teammate Yogi Berra to replace him. In turn, Berra asked Ford to become the team's first pitching coach-player. Wishing to do anything he could to help his friend succeed in his new position, Ford eagerly agreed. But as the year wore on, signs of the team's decline were showing. By 1964, star players like Maris and Mantle were beginning to show their age.

In spite of age and fear of injury, the Yankees took the American League pennant again that autumn of 1964, and were once more in the World Series. This time they faced the St. Louis Cardinals. As he had done so many times before, Ford was named starting pitcher for Game 1. He was doing well up until the sixth inning, with the Yankees scoring 4 runs to the Cardinals' 2, but then something distressing happened. On the mound for the Yankees, Ford was getting ready to pitch another ball and suddenly he couldn't pick it up. Numbness spread throughout his throwing arm. Unable to pitch, he was taken out of the game. At first, doctors in the team's clubhouse thought Ford was having a heart attack. Then he was diagnosed with circulatory problems. Ford couldn't pitch the rest of the series, which went to seven games. Unfortunately, the Yankees lost. Several days later Berra was fired as the team's manager. A year of high expectations had ended on a low point. And although he didn't know it at the time, Ford would never pitch in a World Series game again.

The team started to fall apart after that year. Ford's circulatory problem, partially

Ford poses with a ball marked to signify that he is playing in his twelfth World Series. He made a record 22 major league World Series starts, pitching against the St. Louis Cardinals on October 7, 1964.

treated with surgery, would not allow him the flexibility and control which he had previously known. Batting stars Mantle and Maris were both injured, and the Yankees finished in sixth place, twenty-five games out of first place. It was the team's first losing season since 1925. In 1966, Ford had another, more involved operation on his arm, which turned out to be a success. He had to stay out the remainder of the season to recover.

Ultimately, the Yankees played as badly as they had the year before. Berra's replacement, John Keane, was fired, and former manager Ralph Houk came back to take the reins.

Ford's health problems were not over, however. He developed a bone spur in his left elbow, making pitching more and more painful. He wrote later in *Slick*, "Sooner or later the arm goes bad. It has to . . . Sooner or later you have to start pitching in pain." By May of 1967, Ford could no longer pitch a full inning. It felt as if his elbow were on fire when he tried throwing a ball. At his last game in Detroit against the Tigers, he walked off the mound at the end of the first inning, got dressed, and left the ballpark. On manager Houk's locker Ford left a note. "DEAR RALPH. I'VE HAD IT. CALL YOU WHEN I GET HOME. WHITEY." At the age of thirty-eight, the legend had walked off the field and retired.

Paying tribute to the left-hander, Mickey Mantle once revealed, as it was recorded in the *Baseball Almanac*, why the Yankees knew they

Teammate Mickey Mantle watches as Ford bids farewell to the game at Yankee Stadium on May 30, 1967, prior to the start of a doubleheader against the Minnesota Twins.

could rely on Ford. "I don't care what the situation was, how high the stakes were—the bases could be loaded and the pennant riding on every pitch, it never bothered Whitey. He pitched his game. Cool. Craft. Nerves of steel."

8 Retirement

After his official retirement from the Yankees in May 1967, Whitey Ford was unsure of what path to follow. He still needed to support his family, and he thought that the Yankees organization, now owned by the television studio CBS, would pay him until the end of the season. He was mistaken, however. The Yankees provided only two weeks' severance pay for the pitching veteran. But in 1968, Ford's old friend Ralph Houk, now back in the Yankee front office, offered him a job as first-base coach for the team. At the time Ford knew nothing but baseball. His three children had grown into teenagers, and he now faced the prospect of their expensive college fees. Even though Ford did not think he would make a good coach, he took the job anyway. One of the perks of returning to the team was that he could see his good friend Mickey Mantle more often. Despite various injuries and a decline in his batting abilities, Mantle was still an active player. But Ford was dismayed to see how much Mantle struggled to keep up. He often recalled how difficult it was to witness firsthand the decline of Mantle's ability as a ballplayer. Mantle did retire that year, with 536 home runs for his career, making it to fourth place on the all-time list.

It took just one year as first-base coach for Ford to discover that it was not what he wanted to do with the rest of his life. He didn't return to the Yankees in 1969, but spent the next six years pursuing various interests, most of which he admitted were somewhat aimless. Ford kept in close contact with many of his fellow players and other members of the Yankees organization anyway, and it was no surprise to see him at a Yankees game every once in a while. Always in attendance at the annual Old Timers Day celebrations at Yankee Stadium, Ford worked for a while as a television commentator for Yankee home games.

After his retirement from baseball, Ford took up a number of hobbies, including horse racing. Here he drives a pacer named Tarport Birdie at Pompano Park in Pompano Beach, Florida, in April 1969.

Back to the Bench

It wasn't until 1973 that a chance meeting with new principal Yankees owner George Steinbrenner at the staff Christmas party presented Ford with the opportunity to rejoin the Yankees' coaching staff. Steinbrenner, who said that Ford had been away too long, asked him to rejoin the Yankees' organization. After the New Year's holiday had passed, Ford was asked by the Yankees' general manager, Gabe Paul, to think about becoming the club's pitching coach. The opportunity couldn't have come at a better time. Ford had made a number of bad investments and needed to increase his income. Perhaps more important, he missed being away from baseball and the excitement and competitive spirit it provided. He agreed to return to the Yankees and negotiated a contract to begin coaching in the spring of 1974.

During that time, Yankee Stadium was undergoing renovations, and the team had worked out an agreement to share space with the New York Mets at Shea Stadium in Queens. Ford reported for coaching duty there, a quick trip from his home in Long Island. He enjoyed his work, encouraging younger pitchers and giving them inside hints and pointers that he had acquired from his years of experience. During home games, he sat on the bench next to the manager, Bill Virdon, and studied his pupils. The Yankees didn't make it to the World Series that year, but Ford felt that the team had done its best. And the Yankees organization believed that Ford had contributed to the team's skills.

That same year, the team retired Ford's uniform number 16 in honor of the many victories he had secured for the Yankees. Ford joined the ranks of Babe Ruth, Lou Gehrig, Joe DiMaggio, and his great friend Mickey Mantle, all of whom had their uniform numbers retired. But among them, Ford was the only pitcher that the Yankees had honored in this way. Ford remembered it fondly.

The year was not to end, however, without one more award for the now famous left-hander. On August 11, 1974, in Cooperstown, New York, Ford and his friend and teammate Mickey Mantle were inducted into the Hall of Fame. It was unusual for teammates to be inducted together, and only four pairs of players from the same team have been inducted in the same year. But Ford and Mantle were unique—a winning team. Ford did not expect this honor, however. The year before was the first he had been eligible for induction, and he did not receive the required 75 percent of the votes. As it happened, Mickey Mantle's first year of eligibility for induction was Ford's

Baseball Hall of Famers pose with their plaques. Standing from left to right are Mickey Mantle and Whitey Ford. Seated are James Bell and Joco Conlan.

second, and they both got in together. "For us to get in at the same time, as close as we were, after all we had been through together . . . well, that just made it that much more special," said Ford joyfully in *Slick*.

The families of both men attended the event. Ford's wife, Joan, and their daughter Sally Ann, now married, were in attendance. Ford's sons Tommy and Eddie, now a minor league baseball player with the Boston Red Sox, also came to pay tribute to the Yankee pair. Other famous former players, like Joe DiMaggio, Satchel Paige, and Ford's old manager Casey Stengel showed up for the private dinner before the ceremonies. Ford and Mantle were presented with special Hall of Fame rings marking their induction into the baseball shrine. For Ford, this was the best part of the Hall of Fame weekend, a time that he could spend with his old friends. They just sat around remembering old times, eating, and generally having a great time. For a kid from Queens who never really thought he could have it all, it was a dream come true. "Being elected to the Hall of Fame is, without a doubt, the highlight of my career. But it never was anything I imagined was possible," Ford recalled happily in *Slick*.

Health Scares and Another Career

Going into the 1975 season, Ford looked forward to working with a good team and possibly winning enough games to capture the American League pennant. Instead, he had to leave the team in May.

One warm humid day, Ford and the team started batting practice for that night's game in New York. Ford, who was standing on the pitcher's mound, suddenly felt dizzy. He darted back to the clubhouse but before he could make it, he fell down unconscious. Rushed to the hospital with chest pains, Ford stayed under the watchful eyes of doctors. After a few weeks he was discharged. A cardiologist, who also happened to be an old teammate of Ford's, recommended that he cut down on his strenuous work habits to avoid any more visits to the hospital. Ford agreed. His days as an official Yankee pitching coach were now over.

Ford stretches out before instructing pitchers during spring training drills at the Yankees' camp in Tampa, Florida, on February 23, 1996.

These days, Ford is still able to maintain a busy schedule. He still goes to Yankee spring training every year, looking over the pitching recruits and appraising their prospects for the coming season. Sadly, he missed spring training in early 2000 because he was completing radiation treatment for an undisclosed form of cancer. "While the schedule of those treatments kept me from attending spring training in February, I feel great and have resumed my full schedule of commitments and activities," he said in a recent press release. Previously, Ford had had a brush with cancer in 1994. At the time he underwent hours of surgery to remove a cancerous tumor from behind his ear.

But by August 2000, Ford was looking and feeling fine as the guest of honor on Whitey Ford Day at Yankee Stadium. Celebrating fifty years as a Yankee, Ford was presented with gifts like a car and a trip to the Bahamas. Fellow Hall of Famers and Yankee players Yogi Berra and Phil Rizzuto were among the guests at the ceremony. Speaking before the start of a game between the Yankees and the Anaheim Angels, Ford told the

Yankee legends Yogi Berra and Whitey Ford salute the flag during Old Timers Day ceremonies at Yankee Stadium on July 21, 2001.

crowd, "I haven't been this nervous since I pitched against Ted Williams [a batter for the Boston Red Sox] for the first time!"

In addition to his involvement at spring training, Ford serves as an unofficial ambassador for the Yankees organization, sometimes standing in for George Steinbrenner or other Yankee executives at social functions and charity events. He also has his own charity—the Whitey Ford Children's Foundation—that raises money for distribution to various needy causes.

Ford is the author of a number of books as well, the newest of which is called *Few and Chosen: Defining Yankee Greatness Across the Eras*. In the book, he lists his five top Yankee players for each baseball position, modestly omitting himself. Making comparisons between the baseball players of today and of the past, Ford says that contemporary players are stronger. He also says that batters rack up more home runs than in the past due to thinner bat handles that allow today's bats to generate incredible speeds.

National Baseball Hall of Fame and Museum

The National Baseball Hall of Fame and Museum is a major tourist attraction and is considered a sports shrine by baseball fans throughout the world.

Located in Cooperstown, New York, the National Baseball Hall of Fame and Museum is one of baseball's most visited and well-known attractions. The Hall of Fame was originally conceived as an exhibit featuring a baseball used by the game's founder, Abner Doubleday, and owned by Stephen C. Clark, a Cooperstown resident. Interest in baseball memorabilia, along with a desire to pay tribute to some of baseball's heroes, led to the development of the National Baseball Hall of Fame and Museum. Ford Frick, president of the National League;

William Harridge, president of the American League; Kennesaw Mountain Landis, the first commissioner of baseball; as well as Clark and his associate Alexander Cleland are credited with the startup of the baseball shrine. Officially opened in June 1939, the Hall of Fame commemorated the 100th anniversary of baseball, honored great players, and displayed heirlooms from baseball's history. Members of the Baseball Writers' Association of America were asked by the hall's founders to nominate players to the Hall of Fame's list of outstanding athletes. Among the first inductees to the Hall of Fame was Yankees player Babe Ruth.

Besides being honored by the Yankees, Ford had a playing field in Queens named in his honor. In 2001, the city of New York and then-Mayor Rudolph Giuliani paid tribute to Ford as one of baseball's greats and allowed him to select a site that would bear his name. If you go to the playing field at 26th Avenue and First Street in Astoria, you can see Whitey Ford Field at Hellgate Park. A true New York sports legend, Ford has inspired generations of boys and girls who have baseball dreams of their own.

Election to the Hall of Fame is based upon the player's record in the major leagues, as well as his playing ability, integrity, sportsmanship, character, and contributions to the team or teams on which he played. Currently, there are 254 members. They range from pitchers Whitey Ford and Nolan Ryan, to outfielders Reggie Jackson and Dave Winfield, to catchers Yogi Berra and Johnny Bench. Whitey Ford and Mickey Mantle are among the four pairs of teammates picked by baseball writers to join the Hall of Fame in the same year.

In addition to the Hall of Fame Gallery, where plaques of every Hall of Famer are on view, there are exhibits featuring specific aspects of baseball such as records set in the game. The Hall of Fame presents an annual salute to the current World Series champion team, with photos, baseball gear, and other souvenirs. An exhibit entitled "Ballparks" features actual seats, turnstiles, and dugout benches from landmark parks like the New York Polo Grounds and Brooklyn's Ebbets Field.

Whitey Ford Records

When he retired, Whitey Ford held eight World Series pitching records, as shown in the table below. He also held several other distinctions, such as pitching 33 consecutive scoreless innings during the 1960, 1961, and 1962 World Series (breaking Babe Ruth's record of 29 innings), and ranking second in shutouts (3) and fourth in complete games (7).

Number of wins:	10	Games pitched:	22
Innings pitched:	146	Most walks:	34
Strikeouts:	94	Most series played by a pitcher:	11
Hits allowed:	132		
Number of losses:	8		

The Hall of Fame's Timeline provides a history of baseball complete with highlights of each era. Among the exhibit's many artifacts are Mickey Mantle's baseball bat, a locker used by Joe DiMaggio, and a warm-up jacket worn by Jackie Robinson. There are also examples of old and new baseball equipment in the exhibit as well as a collection of uniforms from the early woolen flannels to today's synthetic outfits.

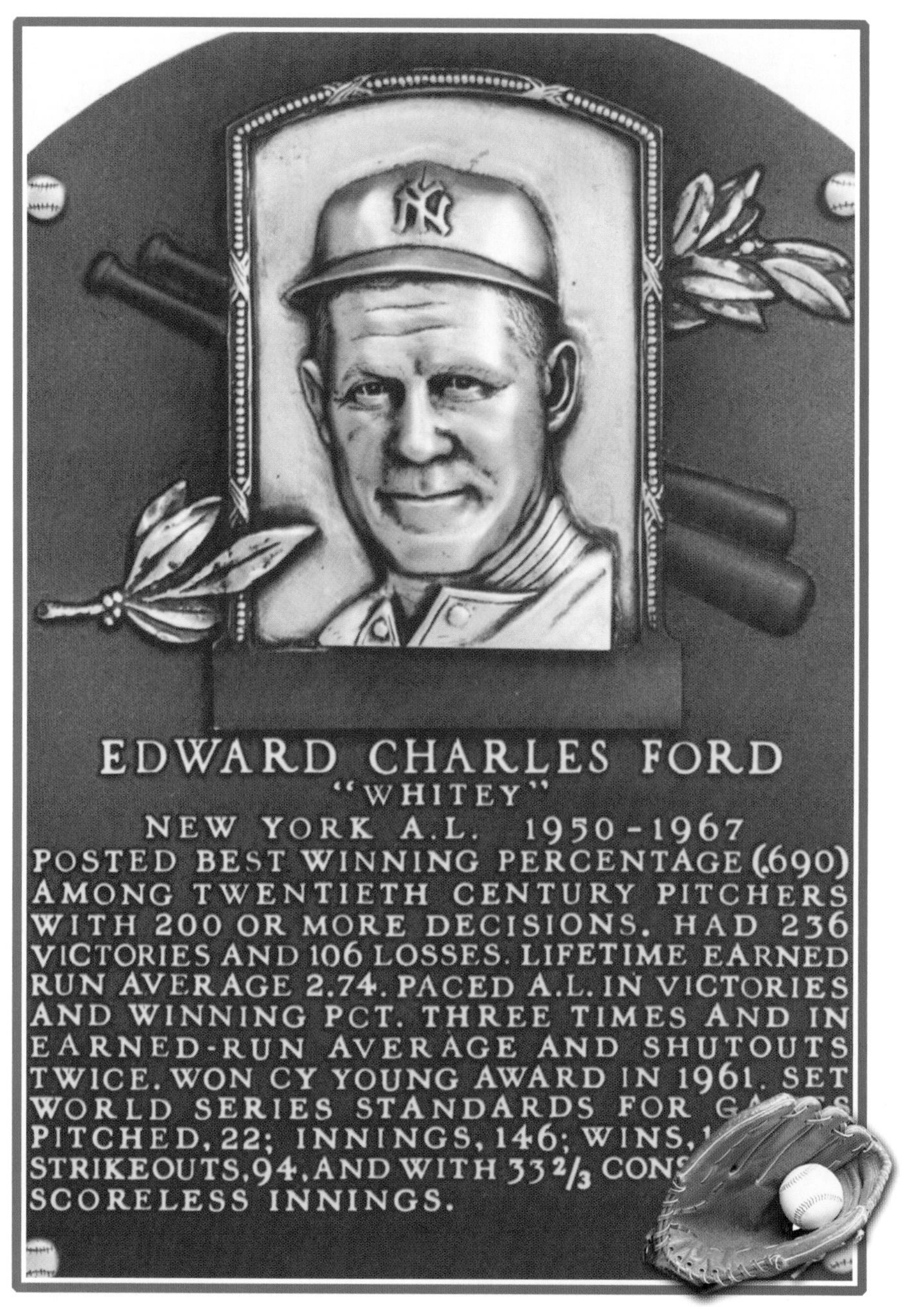

This is Whitey Ford's plaque at the National Baseball Hall of Fame in Cooperstown, New York.

Aside from World Series records, Ford's career statistics of 236 wins and 106 losses gave him a winning percentage of .690—the third best in major league baseball history, and the best of the twentieth century among players with 200 or more decisions.

Each year the Hall of Fame Weekend welcomes fans to the annual Hall of Fame induction ceremony. If you are interested in this event, or would like to know more about the Hall of Fame, note the address in the For More Information section of this book.

WHITEY FORD *TIMELINE*

Oct. 21, 1928	Edward Charles Ford is born in New York City during the Great Depression.
1941	Ford and his teenage friends organize the Thirty-fourth Avenue Boys, an amateur neighborhood baseball team.
1947	Although several major league teams show interest in Ford's ability as a ballplayer, he joyfully signs with the New York Yankees.
1948	Ford is sent to the Yankees Class B team in Norfolk, Virginia.
1950	Ford heads to Yankee spring training, joining players such as Joe DiMaggio and Yogi Berra. He acts as the Yankees' starting pitcher that same season and plays in his first World Series.
1951	Ford marries his longtime girlfriend, Joan Foran, on April 14, to the delight of his Yankee teammates.
1957	Ford's major league performance hits a low point. The Giants and the Dodgers leave New York for the West Coast.

1961	Ford breaks Babe Ruth's record for consecutive scoreless innings in a World Series, extending the streak to 33 scoreless innings.
1963	Ford becomes the Yankees' first coach-player, yet the team suffers new losses.
1964	Unable to pitch due to sudden numbness in his arm, Ford is taken out of the 1964 World Series and diagnosed with circulatory problems.
1967	Unable to continue pitching, Ford retires by simply walking of the field mid-game.
1968	Ford attempts a position as a Yankees' first-base coach.
1969	Leaving the Yankees once again, Ford pursues various interests over the next several years.
1973	Ford returns to the Yankees, this time as the teams pitching coach. His number, 16, is retired.
Aug. 11, 1974	Ford is inducted into the National Baseball Hall of Fame.

Glossary

All-Star Game A game played between the two all-star teams in the middle of the baseball season.

amateur A person with little to no experience in a particular profession or job.

American League One of the two major professional U.S. baseball leagues, established in 1900. The American and the National Leagues are each made up of three divisions: East, Central, and West.

batting average An average determined by dividing the number of base hits by the number of official times at bat. The result is carried to three decimal places. A player with 100 base hits in 300 times at bat has a batting average of .333.

cardiologist A medical doctor who specifically studies the heart and its functions.

curveball A medium-speed pitch that drops several inches as it approaches home plate.

double A hit that results in the batter safely reaching second base.

draft To choose new players from a pool of talented prospects; to require a man to enter into military service.

error A fielding mistake made during a game by a player or team.

farm team A team in a system designed to train young players for the major leagues. Every major league has a farm-club arrangement.

fastball The most common pitch, normally thrown between eighty-five and ninety-five miles per hour. Batters can be confused between fastballs and changeups, which are thrown at the same motion as fastballs, but travel at a much slower speed.

Great Depression A period of United States history, from the stock market crash of 1929 to 1941, of low economic activity marked by rising levels of unemployment.

home run A hit that allows the batter to reach home plate safely and score a run. Most home runs are hit out of the field of play, but a hitter can also run around the bases to home plate before being tagged with the baseball.

National League The older of the two major professional U.S. baseball leagues; it was established in 1876.

pennant In baseball, the flag that represents a league championship; the championship itself.

pitching rotation A team's starting pitchers and the order in which they appear in games.

rookie A first-year baseball player.

roster A list of players on a team.

severance pay An allowance, usually based on length of service, that is payable to an employee on termination of employment.

thwart To oppose successfully.

triple-A The highest class of minor league baseball, followed by double-A and single-A.

veteran A person with great and long-term experience at an occupation or skill.

World Series An annual series of up to seven games between the winning teams of the two major baseball leagues; the first team to win four games becomes champion of major league baseball.

For More Information

The National Baseball Hall of Fame
and Museum
25 Main Street
P.O. Box 590
Cooperstown, NY 13326
(888) 425-5633
Web site:
http://www.baseballhalloffame.org

The New York Yankees
Yankee Stadium
161st Street and River Avenue
Bronx, NY 10452
Web site: http://newyork.yankees.mlb.com

Society for American Baseball Research
812 Huron Road, Suite 719
Cleveland, OH 44115
(216) 575-0500
Web site: http://www.sabr.org

Web Sites

Due to the changing nature of Internet links, the Rosen Publishing Group, Inc., has developed an online list of Web sites related to the subject of this book. This site is updated regularly. Please use this link to access the list:

http://www.rosenlinks.com/bhf/wfor

For Further Reading

Goodman, Michael E. *The New York Yankees* (Baseball). Mankato, MN: Creative Paperbacks, Inc., 2002.

Grabowski, John F. *The New York Yankees* (Great Sports Teams). Farmington Hills, MI: Gale/Lucent Books: 2001.

Joseph, Paul. *New York Yankees* (America's Game). Mankato, MN: Abdo and Daughters, 1997.

Pietrusza, David. *The New York Yankees Baseball Team* (Great Sports Teams). Berkeley Heights, NJ: Enslow Publishers, 1998.

Rambeck, Richard. *The History of the New York Yankees* (Baseball). Mankato, MN: Creative Education, 1998.

Bibliography

Ford, Whitey, and Phil Pepe. *Slick: My Life in and Around Baseball*. New York: Dell Publishers, 1988.

Gutman, Bill. *Modern Baseball Superstars*. New York: Dodd, Mead & Co., 1973.

Hano, Arnold. *A Day in the Bleachers*. New York: Da Capo Press, 1982.

Lally, Richard. *Bombers: An Oral History of the Yankees*. New York: Crown Publishers, 2002.

Robinson, Ray, and Christopher Jennison. *Pennants and Pinstripes: The New York Yankees, 1903–2002*. New York: Viking Press, 2002.

Index

G

H

I

J

K

L

M

N

O

P

Q

Photo Credits

Cover, pp. 4, 23, 33, 36, 68, 77, 79, 82, 88, 96 © AP/Wide World Photos; p. 6 © Topps Company; pp. 8, 39, 42, 46, 50–51, 54, 57, 60, 64, 65, 74, 85 © Bettmann/Corbis; pp. 10, 20 © Hulton Archive/Getty Images; pp. 12–13 © Joel Yale/TimePix; pp. 16–17 © Underwood & Underwood/Corbis; pp. 26–27 © Mark Kauffman/TimePix; p. 90 © Reuters NewMedia Inc./Corbis; p. 92 © Bob Rowan/Progressive Image/Corbis.

Editor

Joann Jovinelly

Series Design and Layout

Geri Giordano